SPECIAL BONUS!

Want These 2 Books For <u>FREE</u>?

 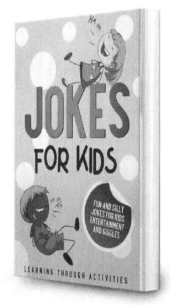

Get <u>FREE</u>, unlimited access to these and all of our new kids books by joining our community!

Scan W/ Your Camera To Join!

Table of Contents

Introduction

Origami is the art of transforming a sheet of paper in this case a dollar bill! This must be done without using instruments such as scissors or glue.

Creating origami helps improve concentration, abstract thinking, fine-motor skills and hand-eye coordination, all while promoting creativity.

In 'Dollar Bill Origami For Kids' you will find 20 impressive designs to immerse yourself in this new wonderful hobby. The book starts with easier dollar bill designs and get more challenging as you go through it!

Are you ready to impress your friends and family with cool amazing dollar bill designs? Let the fun begin!

Symbols

Lines

– – – – – – – – – –   Valley fold, fold forward.

· · · · · · · · · · · · · · · · ·   Mountain fold, a backward.

———————————   Crease line

Arrows

Fold in this direction.

Turn over.

Shows the result after each step.

Dollar Bill

2

Heart

Step 1

Fold the bill in half
lengthwise and unfold it.

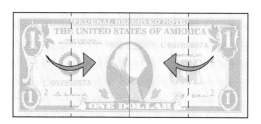

Step 2

Fold both sides in
towards the center
crease you just made.

Step 3

Flip the bill over and fold both
bottom corners up as shown.

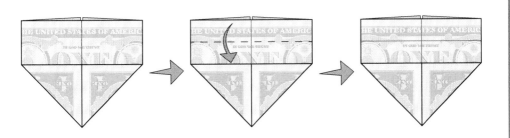

<Step 4>

Fold the top edge of the top layer of the bill down
and unfold it to make a crease.

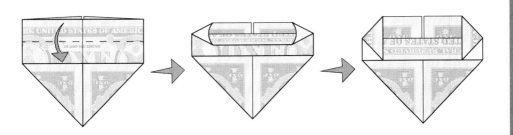

<Step 5>

Fold the top edge of the top layer of the bill down
and flatten the corners as shown.

Step 6

After step 5, you will see two corners right in the center of the bottom layer. Fold them forwards and down as shown.

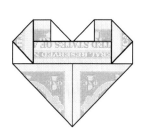  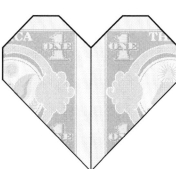

Step 7

Flip the figure over.

Heart

Swan

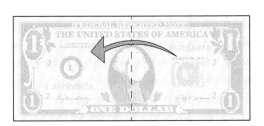

Fold the bill in half lengthwise and unfold it to make a crease.

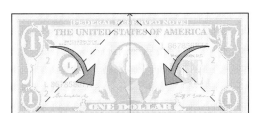

Step 2

Fold both top corners down so that their top edge ends up matching the vertical crease from previous step.

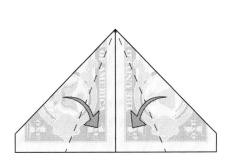

Step 3

Fold both sides again toward the vertical mid line, then rotate the figure so its tip ends up pointing to the left.

Swan

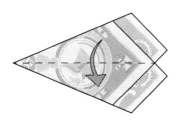 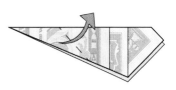

<< Step 4 >>

Fold the figure in half

<< Step 5 >>

Fold the left corner up
as shown and unfold to
make a crease.

<< Step 6 >>

Use the crease from the previous
step to make an outside reverse
fold on the left corner.

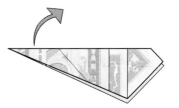

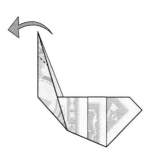

<< Step 7 >>

Then make another outside
reverse fold on the tip as
shown to make the swan's head.

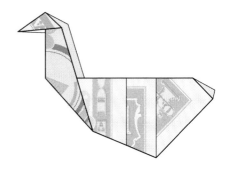

<< Swan >>

Pigeon

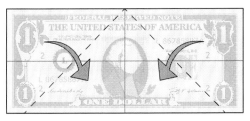

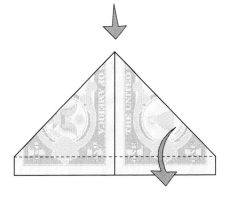

Step 1

Fold the bill in half lengthwise and crosswise and unfold it to make a crease.

Step 2

Fold both top corners down so that their top edge ends up matching the center vertical crease from previous step.

Step 3

Fold the excess part backward and unfold it to make a crease.

Pigeon

Step 4

Fold both edges inward
on the crease you
just made.

Step 5

Fold the bill along those
diagonals again to make
a triangle.

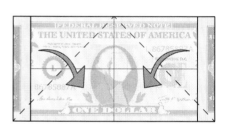

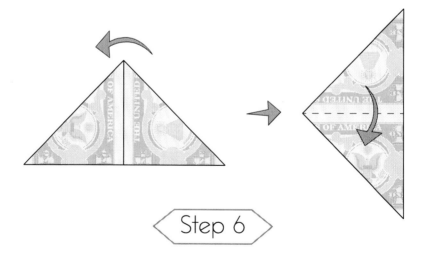

Step 6

Rotate the figure to the left and fold it down in half.

Pigeon

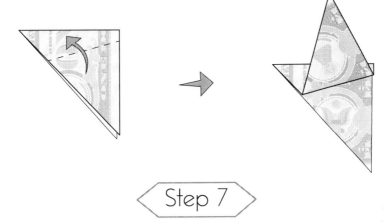

Fold the top layer back up a shown, then do the same on the other side of the figure.

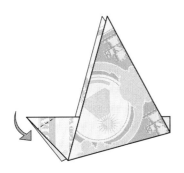

Step 8

Make an inside reverse fold on the left tip of the bill to make the pigeon's beak.

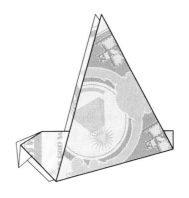

Pigeon

10

Rocket

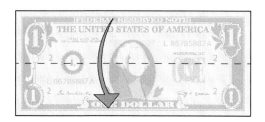

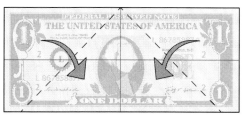

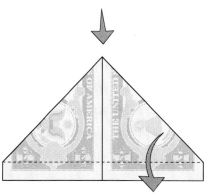

Step 1

Fold the bill in half crosswise and lengthwise and unfold it make a crease.

Step 2

Fold both top corners down so that their top edge ends up matching the vertical crease from the previous step.

Step 3

Fold both bottom excess edges backward and unfold it to make a crease.

Rocket

Step 4

Now fold both edges inward on the crease you made in previous step.

Step 5

Fold the bill along those diagonals again to make a triangle.

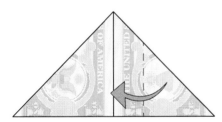

Step 6

Fold the right corner inward as shown.

Step 7

Fold it back outward leaving a small gap between the two folds as shown.

Rocket

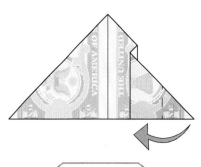

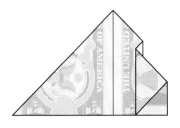

Step 8

Fold the right corner
again until its tip matches
the fold from the
previous step.

Step 9

Repeat the same
for the other side
and match the illustration.

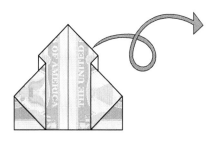

Step 10

Flip the figure over.

Rocket

Car

Step 1

Fold the bill lengthwise
and unfold. Then fold both
sides in towards the center
line you just made.

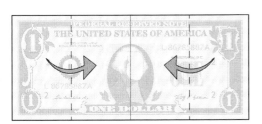

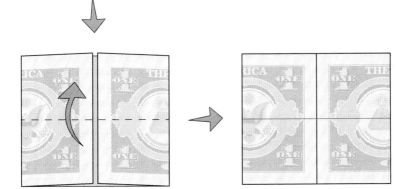

Step 2

Fold the bill in half crosswise and unfold it.

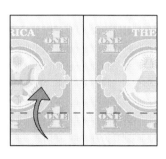

Step 3

Bring the bottom edge forward
to that crease.

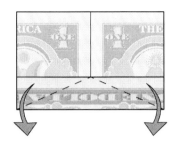

Step 4

Fold both bottom corners
down as shown.

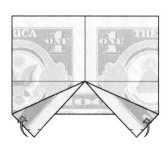

Step 5

Fold the tips of the flaps you
just made back up.

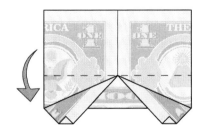

Step 6

Then fold the top half of the
figure down.

 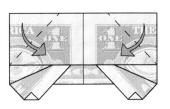

Step 7

Fold the top half back up, but leaving a small gap at the top.

Step 8

Fold both top corners down as shown.

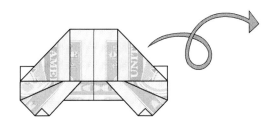

Step 9

Flip the figure over.

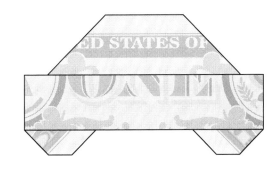

Car

Shirt

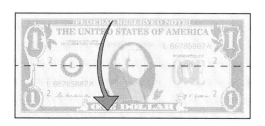

Fold the bill in half
crosswise and unfold.

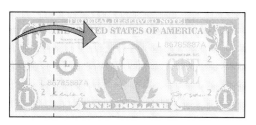

Step 2

Fold the left edge inward.

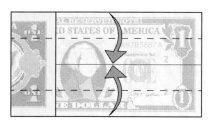

Step 3

Bring the top and bottom edges
forward toward the center crease
from Step 1.

Shirt

Step 4

Fold the flaps on the left side out as shown. These will be sleeves of the shirt.

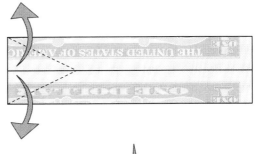

Step 5

Fold the right edge backward as shown.

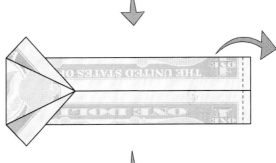

Step 6

Fold the tip of the right corners backward to make the collar of the shirt.

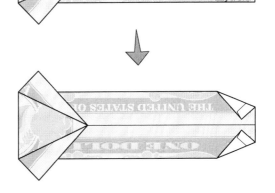

Shirt

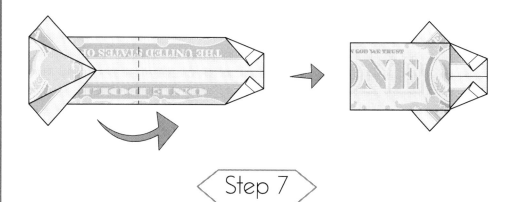

Fold the left side of the figure over the right side. Tuck the top layer under it as shown.

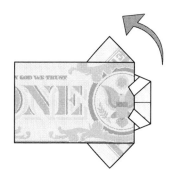

Step 8

Rotate the figure.

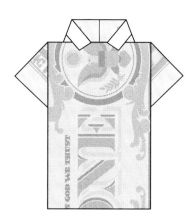

Shirt

Step 1

Fold the bill in half lengthwise and crosswise and unfold it to make a crease.

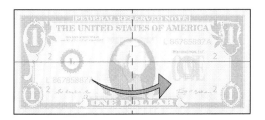

Step 2

Bring the top and bottom edges forward toward the center crease you just made.

Step 3

Fold the bill lengthwise as shown.

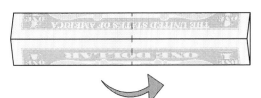

Pants

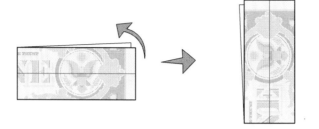

Rotate the figure until the fold from the previous step sits at the bottom and the free edges are at the top.

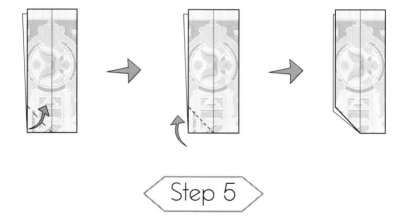

Fold the bottom left corner up and unfold it, then use that crease to tuck the corner between both layers of the bill.

Pants

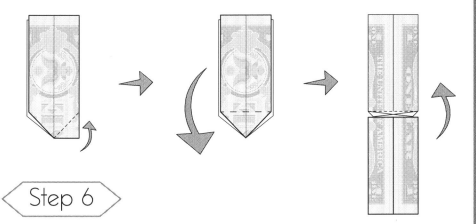

Step 6

Repeat with the lower right corner.

Step 7

Fold the top layer down leaving a triangle under the flap that you are going t make as shown. Flip the shape over and repeat with the other side of the bill.

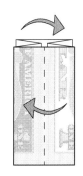

Step 8

Fold the top layer in half, then flip the figure over and do the same with the other side.

Pants

Diamond

Fold the bill in half lengthwise and unfold.

Fold both top corners down so that their top edge ends up matching the vertical crease from the previous step.

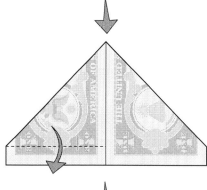

Fold the bottom edge of the left flap inward to match the bottom layer to make a crease and unfold. Now unfold the left flap completely.

Diamond

Step 4

Fold the edge back in along the crease you just made.

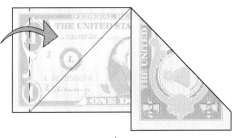

Step 5

Fold the top left corner back down along the crease from step 2.

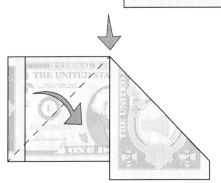

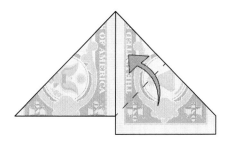

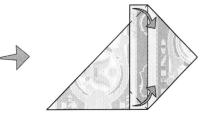

Step 6

Fold the right side up in half as shown.

Step 7

Fold both corners of the top layer inward.

Diamond

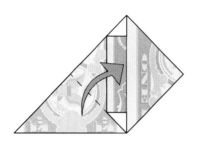 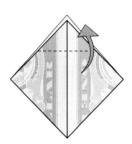

Step 8

Now fold the left side up, slightly overlapping the right side.

Step 9

Then fold the top tip down and tuck it between both layers of the bill.

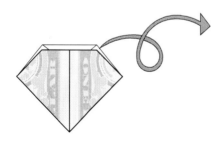

Step 10

Flip the figure over.

Diamond

Fish

Step 1

Fold the bill in half crosswise and unfold it to make a crease.

Step 2

Fold both left corners forward to that crease.

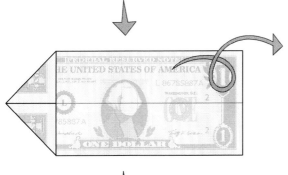

Step 3

Flip the bill over.

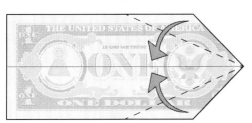

Step 4

Now the corners that you folded in the previous step are on the right side. Fold them forward again to the center crease.

Step 5

Flip the figure over.

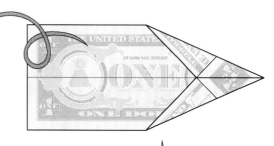

Step 6

Unfold the flaps on the tip of the bill as shown.

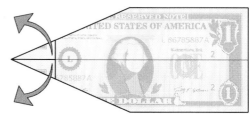

Step 7

Fold the tip of the bill inward to make a triangle.

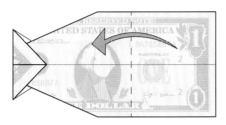 →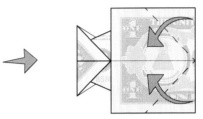

Step 8

Fold the right edge inward
until it meets the tip of
that triangle.

Step 9

Fold both right corners
forward to the center
crease to make a triangle
on the right side of the
bill.

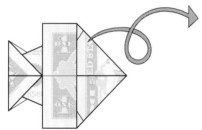

Step 10

Flip the figure over.

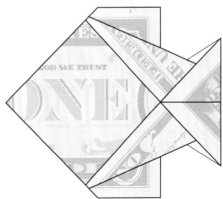

Fish

Santa's Hat

Step 1

Fold the bill in half lengthwise and crosswise and unfold it to make a crease.

Step 2

Bring the left edge to the vertical mid line.

Step 3

Fold both left corners diagonally to make a triangle on that end of the bill.

Santa's Hat

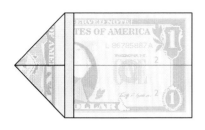 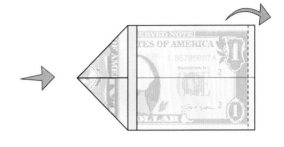

Fold just a little bit of the right edge backward.

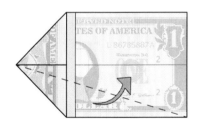 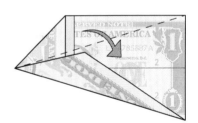

Step 5

Fold the bottom left corner up along the line that joins the tip of the triangle and the bottom right corner.

Step 6

Repeat for the top left corner as shown.

Santa's Hat

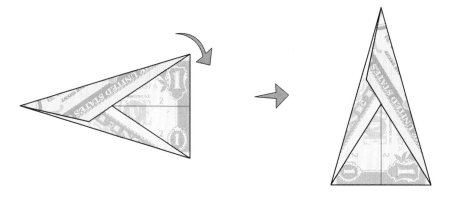

<< Step 7 >>

Rotate the figure so that the tip of the triangle
ends up pointing up.

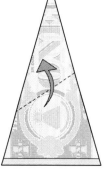

<< Step 8 >>

Fold the figure back roughly
in half with a diagonal
fold as shown.

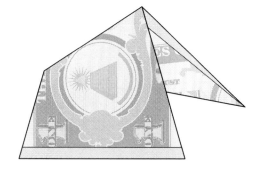

<< Santa's Hat >>

31

Sailboat

Fold the bill in half
lengthwise and unfold.

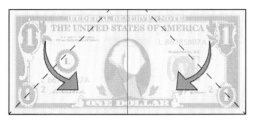

Step 2

Fold both top corners down
toward the bottom edge
of the bill.

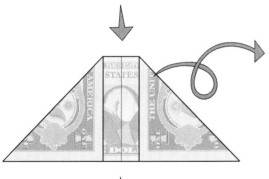

Step 3

Flip the figure over.

Step 4

Fold the right corner up
to the vertical mid line.

Sailboat

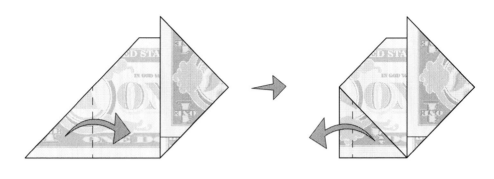

Step 5

Fold the left corner inward
until its tip meets the vertical
mid line.

Step 6

Fold the left corner back
out, leaving a small gap
between the two folds.

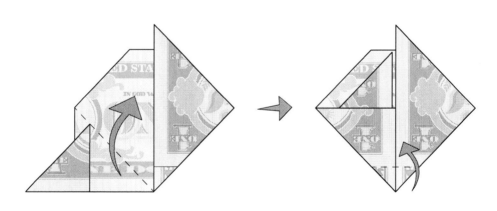

Step 7

Then fold the same corner up
to the vertical mid line as shown.

Step 8

Fold the bottom corner
up as shown.

Sailboat

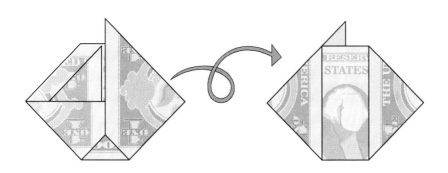

Step 9

Flip the figure over.

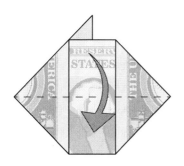

Step 10

Fold the top layer
down in half.

Sail Boat

Bottle

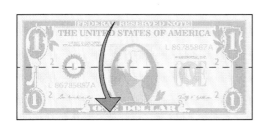

Step 1

Fold the bill in half crosswise and unfold it to make a crease.

Step 2

Bring the top and bottom edges forward toward the crease you just made.

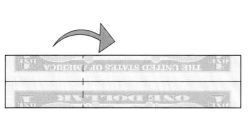

Step 3

Divide the bill into 3 roughly equal parts and fold the left side inward.

Bottle

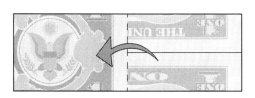 

Step 4

Now fold the right side inward over the left side.

Step 5

Fold the top layer back out, leaving a small gap between the two folds.

Step 6

Fold the top edge of the top layer down to the mid line. As you do it, you'll see the fold from the previous step open up to make a triangle. Flatten it.

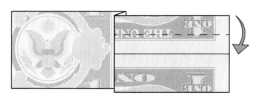

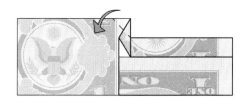

Step 7

Now you can see a corner sticking out. Fold it diagonally down and flatten it.

Bottle

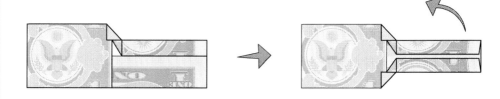

Repeat the steps 6 and 7 for the bottom edge, then rotate the figure until these folds end up pointing up.

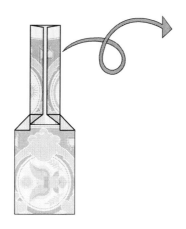

Step 9

Flip the figure over.

Bottle

Step 1

Fold the bill lengthwise and crosswise, then unfold it.

Step 2

Fold the right edge backward to the vertical center line as shown.

Step 3

Fold the top and bottom edges slightly forward and inward as shown.

Step 4

Open the flaps on the right of the top layer and flatten them.

Step 5

Fold the lower right corner forward and up as shown. Repeat for the upper right corner. Make sure both corners overlap.

Step 6

Fold the left edge on top of the right edge.

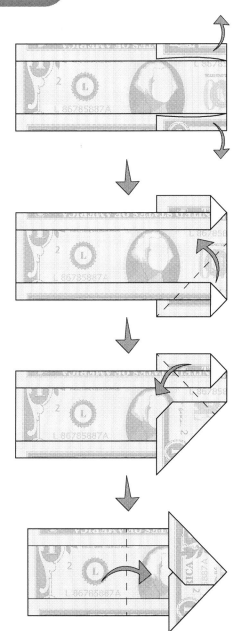

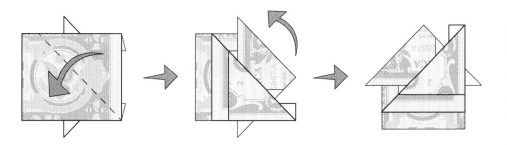

Step 7

Fold the top right corner of the top layer forward an down as shown.

Step 8

Make sure you don't fold the flap you made in step 3 because that will be the chimney. Now rotate the figure as shown.

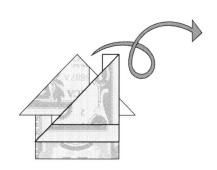

Step 9

Flip the figure over.

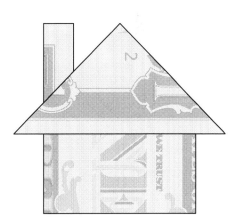

Home

Bell

Step 1

Fold the to left corner down to the bottom edge.

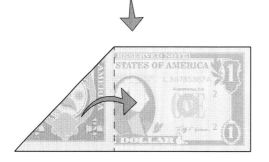

Step 2

Fold the right side of the bill inward along the edge of the flap you just made.

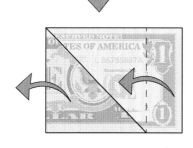

Step 3

Fold the right edge forward at the tip of the fold from the previous step as shown and unfold it.

Step 4

Then fold the right edge on the crease you just made.

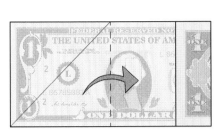

Step 5

Fold the left edge over
the right edge.

Step 6

Rotate the figure until
the folded edge sits
on the top right side.

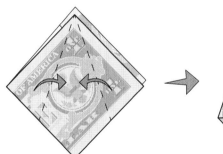

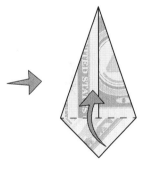

Step 7

Bring both sides in toward the
mid line.

Step 8

Fold the bottom
corner up as shown.

Bell

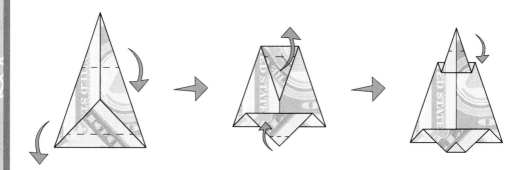

Fold the bottom corner down again, leaving a small gap between the two folds, then fold the tip up again. Fold the top corner down and up again, leaving a small gap between the folds as well. Fold the top tip down as shown.

Flip the figure over.

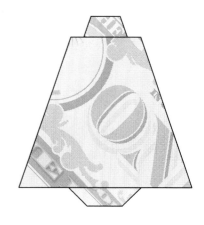

Bell

Gown

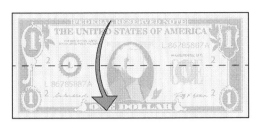

Fold the bill in half crosswise and unfold it to make a crease.

Step 2

Fold the top and bottom edges forward toward the crease you just made and unfold it.

Step 3

Now fold the bill in half lengthwise.

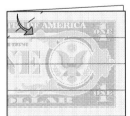

Step 4

Fold the top left corner to make a crease as shown and unfold it.

 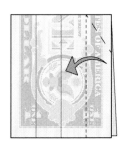

Step 5

Rotate the figure until the fold from the previous step sits at the top and the free edges are at the bottom.

Step 6

Fold the right edge of the top layer in along the creases shown and flatten the top.

Step 7

Do the same for the left side. Flip the figure over.

 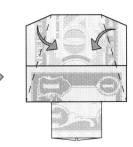 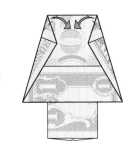

Step 8

Fold up the bottom edge of the top layer.

Step 9

Fold the top corners down as shown.

Step 10

Fold their tips down again.

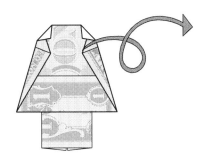

Step 11

Flip the figure over.

Gown

Bow Tie

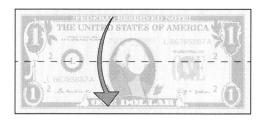

<Step 1>

Fold the bill in half crosswise and unfold. Fold the bill in half lengthwise.

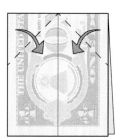

<Step 2>

Rotate the figure until the fold from the previous step sits at the top and the free edges are at the bottom. Then fold both top corners down and unfold them.

Bow Tie

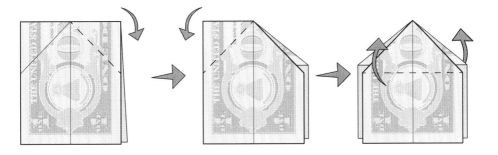

Step 3

Use the right crease to make an inside reverse fold on the right corner. Repeat the same for left corner.

Step 4

Fold up the bottom of the front layer of the bill as shown. Repeat for the back layer.

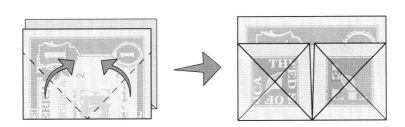

Step 5

Fold both bottom corners up to form a triangle on the front layer. Repeat the same for the other side.

Bow Tie

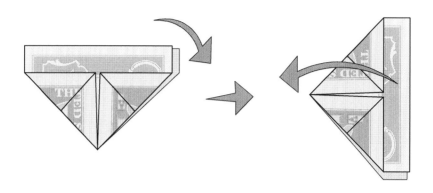

Step 6

Rotate the figure to one of its sides and pull the sides edges apart to separate both layers of the bill.

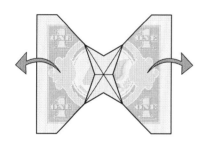

Step 7

While separating both layers, press the center of the figure until it's completely flat.

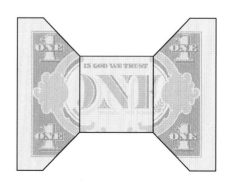

Bow Tie

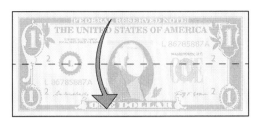

Step 1

Fold the bill in half crosswise and unfold.

Step 2

Fold both left corners diagonally, then unfold them to make a crease.

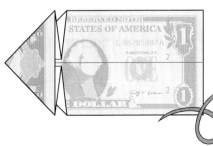

Step 3

Fold the top and bottom edges between the creases from the previous step inward to the center line to make a triangle. Flip the figure over.

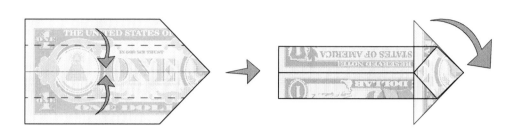

Bring the top and bottom edges forward down to the mid line.
Rotate the bill so the triangle ends up pointing down.

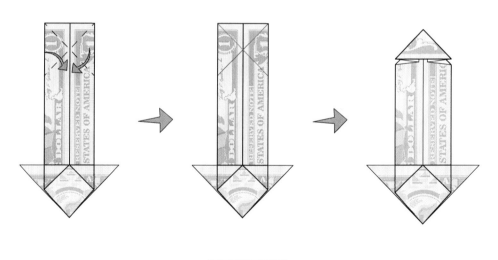

Fold both top corners diagonally down, then unfold them to
make two creases. Repeat the step 3 to make another
triangle on the top edge of the bill.

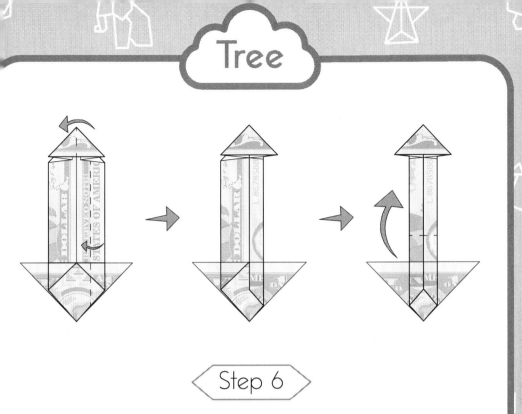

<< Step 6 >>

Then bring both side edges up to the mid line, but make sure to tuck them under the top layer of the triangle you just made. Fold the lower triangle up as shown.

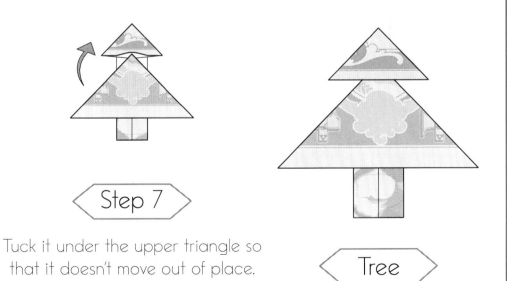

<< Step 7 >>

Tuck it under the upper triangle so that it doesn't move out of place.

<< Tree >>

Wallet

Step 1

Fold the bill in half
lengthwise and crosswise
and unfold it to
make a crease.

Step 2

Fold both top corners down
so that their top edge ends
up matching the vertical
crease from the previous step.
Press and unfold it.

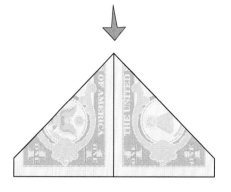

Step 3

Repeat the previous step
for the bottom corners.

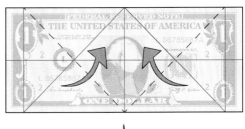

Step 4

Fold both side edges inward
along the line that joins the
creases from step 3 and
4 as shown, then unfold it.

Step 5

Fold both side edges inward
again, this time where the
creases from step 3 and
4 as shown, then unfold it.

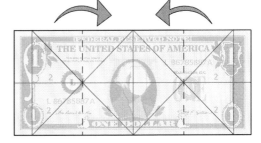

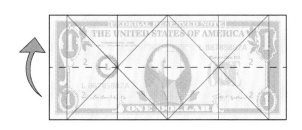

Step 6

Fold the bill up in half crosswise.

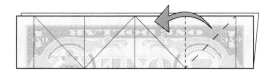

Step 7

Open the right side of the bill by making a vertical valley fold and a diagonal mountain fold at the same time, as shown, to bring the top right corner inward to the vertical mid line. then flatten to make a triangle and flip the figure over.

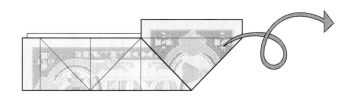

Step 8

Flip the figure over.

Fold the top left corner inward to the mid line as well, and tuck the edge that sticks out at the top between the top layers of the bill.

Step 10

Repeat the previous steps for the other end of the bill.

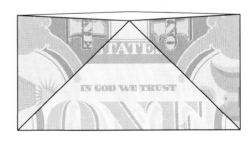

Wallet

Butterfly

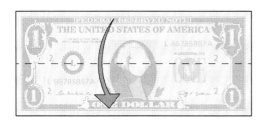

Fold the bill in half crosswise and unfold. Now fold the bill in lengthwise.

Step 2

Rotate the figure until the fold from the previous step sits at the top and the free edges are at the bottom.

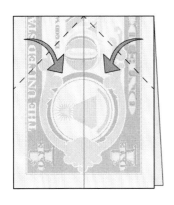 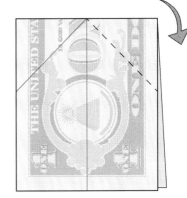

Step 3

Fold both top corners down and unfold them, then use the right crease to make an inside reverse fold on the right corner.

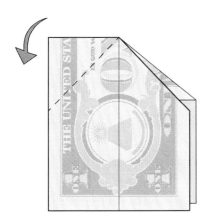 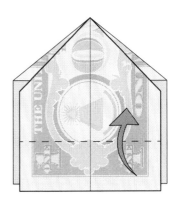

Step 4

Repeat on the left corner to make a triangle on the top side of the bill.

Step 5

Then fold the bottom edge of the top layer backward until it meets that triangle as shown.

Butterfly

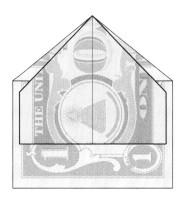 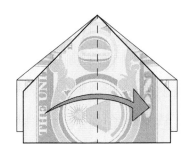

Flip the figure over ad repeat the process for the other side
of the bill. Then fold the top layer in half,
and fold the other side of the bill in half as well.

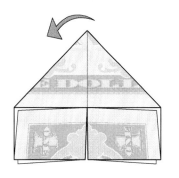 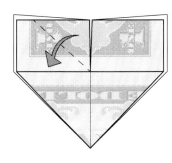

Step 7

You will see that there is a slit in the bottom center of the bill. Turn
the figure upside down and fold the left edge of that slit down
as shown.

Butterfly

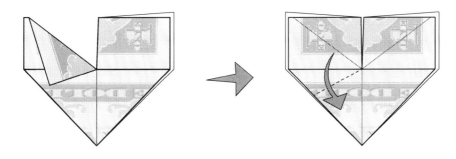

Undo the fold and use that crease to open the flap on the left side and bring it down as you can see in the drawing, then flatten it. This will make on of the butterfly's wings.

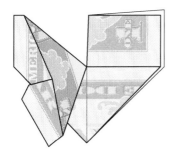

Step 9

Repeat the process on the right side of the figure to make the other wing of the butterfly.

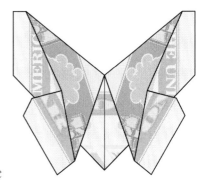

Butterfly

Dog

Fold the top left corner down to the bottom edge.

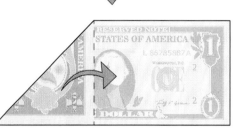

Step 2

Fold the right side of the bill inward along the edge of the flap you just made.

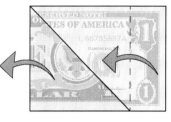

Step 3

Fold the right edge forward at the tip of the fold from the previous step as shown.

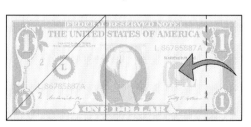

Step 4

Then completely unfold the bill. Fold the right edge on the crease you just made.

Step 5

Now fold the figure in half
as shown.

Step 6

Fold the figure in half
lengthwise and crosswise,
then unfold.

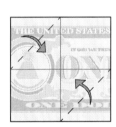  

Step 7

Use those creases
to fold the top left
and bottom right
corners as shown.

Step 8

Fold the tip of the
upper left corner that
you just folded under
itself, and fold the tip
of the bottom right
corner down again.

Step 9

Fold the figure
in half shown.

Dog

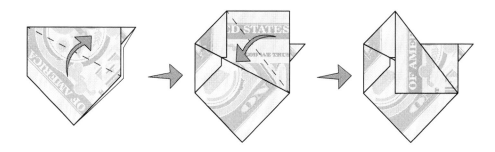

Fold the bottom of
the top layer up
as shown.

Fold it back down as shown.
Repeat for the other side of the bill.

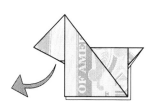

Carefully pull the flap between both
layers and flatten as shown.

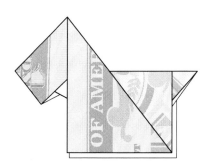

Dog

Conclusion

Congratulations on making it to the end of this origami book. I'm sure you are now a master of the art of folding dollar bills! After learning how to fold animals, objects, and vehicles, try creating some of your own unique designs!

I hope this trip has been fun and you've discovered a new hobby! If you enjoyed this book, we would really appreciate your feed back on amazon, since its our way of learning and growing with you!

Happy Folding!

Made in United States
Orlando, FL
10 December 2024

55321315R00037